Doll A

Doll B

Natalie Wood
Gypsy (1962)
Designer: Orry-Kelly

Betty Grable
Three for the Show (1955)
Designer: Jean Louis

PLATE 1

Norma Shearer
Marie Antoinette (1938)
Designer: Adrian

PLATE 2

Glue to back of head

Leave open

JC

JC

KH

KH

Joan Crawford
The Women (1939)
Designer: Adrian

Katharine Hepburn
The Philadelphia Story (1940)
Designer: Adrian

PLATE 3

Lana Turner
Ziegfeld Girl (1941)
Designer: Adrian

Greta Garbo
Two-Faced Woman (1941)
Designer: Adrian

PLATE 4

Claudette Colbert
The Sign of the Cross (1932)
Designer: Travis Banton

Marlene Dietrich
Shanghai Express (1932)
Designer: Travis Banton

PLATE 5

Carole Lombard
My Man Godfrey (1936)
Designer: Travis Banton

Carmen Miranda
That Night in Rio (1941)
Designer: Travis Banton

PLATE 6

Dolores Del Rio
Wonder Bar (1934)
Designer: Orry-Kelly

Bette Davis
Jezebel (1937)
Designer: Orry-Kelly

PLATE 7

Jack Lemmon
Some Like It Hot (1959)
Designer: Orry-Kelly

Rosalind Russell
Auntie Mame (1958)
Designer: Orry-Kelly

PLATE 8

Marlene Dietrich
Seven Sinners (1940)
Designer: Irene

Lena Horne
As Thousands Cheer (1943)
Designer: Irene

PLATE 9

Lucille Ball
DuBarry Was a Lady (1943)
Designer: Irene

Ann Miller
Easter Parade (1948)
Designer: Irene

PLATE 10

Rita Hayworth
Gilda (1945)
Designer: Jean Louis

Rita Hayworth
Pal Joey (1957)
Designer: Jean Louis

PLATE 11

Glue to back of headdress.

Leave open

JA

JA

Julie Andrews
Thoroughly Modern Millie (1967)
Designer: Jean Louis

PLATE 12

Mae West
She Done Him Wrong (1933)
Designer: Edith Head

Ginger Rogers
Lady in the Dark (1944)
Designer: Edith Head

PLATE 13

Bette Davis
All About Eve (1950)
Designer: Edith Head

Gloria Swanson
Sunset Boulevard (1950)
Designer: Edith Head

PLATE 14

Vivien Leigh
Gone With the Wind (1939)
Designer: Walter Plunkett

Judy Garland
Summer Stock (1950)
Designer: Walter Plunkett

PLATE 15

Debbie Reynolds
Singin' in the Rain (1952)
Designer: Walter Plunkett

Judy Holliday
Bells Are Ringing (1960)
Designer: Walter Plunkett

PLATE 16